PRAYERS AND GRACES

a little book of extraordinary piety

collected by

ALLAN M. LAING

with illustrations by

MERVYN PEAKE

LONDON
VICTOR GOLLANCZ LTD
1944

CONTENTS

ACKNOWLEDGMENTS

FOR PERMISSION TO reprint copyright material, my grateful thanks are due to Mr. Hesketh Pearson (for an extract from *Skye High*); to the Exors. of the late John Sampson, the publishers, Messrs. Chatto and Windus, and the translator (for "Prayer of the Gipsy Modoran" and "Prayer of a Romany Rye" from *The Wind on the Heath*. I have taken the liberty of partly re-writing the second poem); to the Editor of *The Countryman* (for "Crisis in the Nursery"); to Messrs. George Allen and Unwin (for "A Benison on Wartime High Tea," from my own *Bank Holiday on Parnassus*); to the Editor of the *New Statesman and Nation* (for "A Common Grace"); and to Mr. Alasdair Alpin MacGregor (for an extract from *Auld Reekie: Portrait of a Lowland Boyhood*).

I have also to thank Mr. Raymond Mortimer and Professor Graham A. Laing of Pasadena for acquainting me with, respectively, "Nursery Limerick" and "Anecdote for God."

I regret that I have been unable to locate the owner of the copyright in "The Baby's Grace," by the late R. L. Gales. I trust she will accept my apologies for taking permission for granted.

A. M. L.

THE BABY'S GRACE

PRAISE TO GOD who giveth meat
Convenient unto all who eat:
Praise for tea and buttered toast,
Father, Son and Holy Ghost.

R. L. GALES.

A GIPSY BABE'S PRAYER

LITTLE BIRD OF Sparadise,
Do the work of Jesus Chrise:
Go by sea: go by lan':
Go by Goddes holy han'.

PATIENCE DAVIS, *a gipsy.*

5

TOO MUCH RABBIT

FOR RABBITS YOUNG and rabbits old,
For rabbits hot and rabbits cold,
For rabbits tender, rabbits tough,
We thank Thee, Lord: we've had enough.

Attributed to DEAN SWIFT.

THIS PRAYER BUSINESS

THEN MISS WATSON she took me in the closet and prayed, but nothing come of it. She told me to pray every day, and whatever I asked for I would get it. But it warn't so. I tried it. Once I got a fish-line, but no hooks. It warn't any good to me without hooks. I tried for the hooks three or four times, but somehow I couldn't make it work. I asked Miss Watson to try for me, but she said I was a fool. She never told me why, and I couldn't make it out no way.

MARK TWAIN.

RECIPROCITY

HERE LIE I, Martin Elginbrodde:
Hae mercy o' my soul, Lord God,
As I would do, were I Lord God
And Ye were Martin Elginbrodde.

EPITAPH IN ELGIN CATHEDRAL.

STRANGE PETITION

HESKETH PEARSON, joint author with Hugh Kingsmill of *Skye High*, woke up one morning to find himself muttering:

"We earnestly pray Almighty God to persuade the municipal council to give us another poet like Shelley, if he can be spared from the freedom of the seas."

THE ANGLER'S PRAYER

Give me, O Lord, to catch a fish
    So large that even I,
In boasting of it afterwards,
    Shall have no need to lie.

ANON.

COAXING THE DEITY

"O Lord, Thou knowest we are about to have a little bazaar. . . ."

LATE TRADITIONAL.

PRAYER OF THE GIPSY MODORAN

Sweet little God, I beseech thee to grant me everything I ask, because thou art beautiful, high and mighty.

If thou lettest me steal a loaf, brandy, a hen, a goose, a pig or a horse, I will give thee a big candle.

If I have stolen anything, and the Gentiles enter my tent to discover the stolen property, and find nothing, I will give thee two big candles.

If the officers of the law enter my tent, and having searched it and found nothing, depart in peace, I will give thee three big candles.

Because thou art my sweet little golden God.

FROM THE RUMANIAN.

THE CHOSEN GIVE THANKS

SOME HAE MEAT, and canna eat,
  And some wad eat that want it;
But we hae meat, an' we can eat,
  And sae the Lord be thankit.

ROBERT BURNS.

YOU CAN'T PLEASE EVERYBODY

THE DUKE OF RUTLAND urged *The Times* to pray
For rain: the rain came down the following day.
The pious marvelled: sceptics murmured: "Fluke!"
And farmers late with hay said: "Damn that Duke!"

Quoted by E. V. LUCAS.

REBUKE FOR JONES

"FOR WHAT WE ARE about to receive, and for what Mr. Jones has already received, may the Lord make us truly thankful. Amen."

ANON.

MIRACLE WANTED

O LORD, WHO MADE these loaves and fishes,
Look down upon these two poor dishes
And, though they be exceeding small,
Make them enough, we pray, for all;
For if they should our stomachs fill,
Heaven will have wrought a miracle.

ANON.

PRAYER FOR THE PIOUS

Buried in earth or drown'd in th' main,
    Eat up by worms or fishes,
I pray the pious may obtain
    For happy times, their wishes.

THOMAS FULLER.

NO PRAYER FROM THE SCOFFER

T HOUGH TO THE Mosque I come with pious air,
By Allah! think not that I come for prayer;
   I stole a mat once, from a worshipper:
That sin worn out, again I here repair.

OMAR KHAYYÁM.

HARVEST THANKSGIVING

"O LORD, WE THANK Thee for the abundance and safe in-gathering of all our harvest except for a few fields between here and Stonehaven. . . ."

Quoted by DEAN RAMSAY.

AN ANECDOTE FOR GOD

A CURATE, HAVING taken considerable trouble to prepare a speech for a public meeting, found himself, to his disgust, called upon only to lead the audience in prayer. Determined not to waste his material, he embodied most of his speech in his prayer, one passage of which ran:

"Lest this point be too obscure, O Lord, permit Thy servant to illustrate it with an anecdote. . . ."

THE SERVANT MAID'S PRAYER

"O Lord, have I got to get up?"

CRISIS IN THE NURSERY

"Dear Satan, please come for Nurse, and please come soon."

A PARSON-POLITICIAN PRAYS

"O LORD, WE ASK Thee for a Governor who would rule in the fear of God; who would defeat the ringleaders of corruption, enhance the prosperity of the State, promote the happiness of the people—O Lord, what's the use of beating about the bush? Give us George W. Briggs for Governor! Amen."

FATHER TAYLOR.

GENERAL MONTGOMERY GIVES THANKS

"WE MUST NOT FORGET to give thanks to the Lord, 'mighty in battle,' for giving us such a good beginning towards the attainment of our object. . . .

"And now let us get on with the job. Together with our American Allies, we have knocked Mussolini off his perch. We will now drive the Germans from Sicily."

DAILY PRESS (1943).

COME, LET US BARGAIN WITH THE LORD

"LORD, GIVE US GRACE, for if Thou give us not grace, we shall not give Thee glory; and who will win by that, Lord?"

THE REV. MR. HOUSTON.

A BENISON ON WARTIME HIGH TEA

UPON THIS SCANTY meal, O Lord,
Bestow a blessing in accord:
Pour Thy grace in measure small,
Lest it more than cover all.

Bless the tiny piece of ham:
Bless the lonely dab of jam:
Bless the sparsely-buttered toast,
Father, Son and Holy Ghost.

A. M. L.

GRADUATED GRATITUDE

BISHOP WILBERFORCE used to tell the story of a
greedy clergyman who, when asked to say grace, would
look anxiously to see if there were champagne glasses
on the table. If there were, he would begin: "O most
bountiful Jehovah! . . ."; but if he saw only claret glasses,
he would pray: "We are not worthy, O Lord, of these,
the least of Thy mercies. . . ."

PRAYER OF A ROMANY RYE

O MY GOD, to still my longing,
   Give to me a mantle fine,
Gaily trimmed with metal buttons
   In the golden light to shine.

Grant me, too, a goodly wife,
   In her jacket, clean and neat,
Arms of slender willow grace,
   Flowerlike beauty in her feet.

Laughing eyes, like seed of grape,
   Shapely shoulders, like white bread,
Lips as fresh as buds that burst
   Into shining blossoms red.

TRANSYLVANIAN GIPSY SONG.

A DIVINE ADVANTAGE

"LORD, THOU'RT LIKE a wee moosie peepin' oot o' a hole in the wall, for Thou see'st us, but we canna see Thee."

THE REV. MR. HOUSTON.

A LETHAL PRAYER

Dean Inge once received a partly anonymous letter from a lady, who wrote:

"I am praying for your death. I have been very successful in two other instances."

A GRACE FOR LITTLE CHILDREN

Here a little child I stand
Heaving up my either hand;
Cold as paddocks though they be,
Here I lift Them up to Thee,
For a benison to fall
On our meat and on us all.

ROBERT HERRICK.

TRADUTTORE, TRADITORE

A MISSIONARY, WITH A very imperfect knowledge of a certain African dialect, translated the benedictory line, "Lord, dismiss us with Thy blessing," so that it read, in native eyes, "Lord, kick us out softly."

A COMMON GRACE

WE THANK THEE, Lord, for vulgar food,
    For trotters, tripe, pig's cheek,
For steak and onions, with their crude
    But appetising reek.

Potatoes in their jackets make
    Us plain folk honour Thee;
And Thou art with us when we bake
    Fresh shrimps for Sunday tea.

Thy people's praise is overdue,
    But see, dear Lord, we kneel
To offer thanks for Irish stew
    And tasty, cheap cowheel.

Now wait a minute, Lord! Don't miss
    The last word on our lips:
We thank Thee most of all for this,
    Thy gift of fish-and-chips.

A. M. L.

AN ANTI-JACOBITE PRAYS

THE WHIG INCUMBENT of an Edinburgh church did not hesitate to disclose his attitude towards poor Prince Charlie, then holding court at Holyrood: "Bless the King," he prayed. "Thou knowest which King I mean. As for the young man who has come among us to seek an earthly crown, we beseech Thee to take him to Thyself, and bestow on him a crown of glory."

Quoted by ALASDAIR ALPIN MACGREGOR
(in *Auld Reekie: Portrait of a Lowland Boyhood*).

CREATURE COMFORTS

BUT I, WHEN I undress me,
Each night upon my knees,
Will pray the Lord to bless me
With apple-pie and cheese.

ANON. (*American source*).

A GRACE FOR ICE-CREAM

FOR WATER-ICES, cheap but good,
That find us in a thirsty mood;
For ices made of milk or cream
That slip down smoothly as a dream;
For cornets, sandwiches and pies
That make the gastric juices rise;
For ices bought in little shops
Or at the kerb from him who stops;
For chanting of the sweet refrain:
"Vanilla, strawberry or plain?"
  We thank Thee, Lord, who sendst with heat
  This cool deliciousness to eat.

A. M. L.

A NURSERY LIMERICK

THERE ONCE WAS a goose and a wren
Who gave lunch to a cock and a hen:
  "O Lord," prayed the goose,
  "Bless these gifts to our use
And ourselves in Thy service. Amen."

ANON.

IN A MONASTERY BEAR-GARDEN

DEAN SWIFT, BENIGHTED at an Irish monastery, breakfasted next morning—a Friday—on bacon and eggs; but the monks, of course, were having fish. A display of Irish wit followed, the monks leading off with the grace: "From bacon and eggs and rotten legs (Swift was poor on his feet), good Lord deliver us!" Swift immediately countered with: "From oysters and cockles and men without bottles, good Lord deliver us." He followed this up with the lines:

> Does any man of common sense
> Think ham and eggs give God offence?
> Or that a herring has a charm
> The Almighty's anger to disarm?
> Wrapped in His majesty divine,
> D'you think He cares on what we dine?

THE SCOTSMAN'S PRAYER

"O Lord, give us a guid conceit o' oorsel's!"

THE WESSEX PRAYER

God bless me and me wife,
Me son John and his wife,
    Us four:
    No more!

POLISHED PIETY

My soul is like a rusty lock:
    Lord, oil it with Thy grace;
And rub it, rub it, rub it, Lord,
    Until I see Thy face.

                    OLD PURITAN HYMN.

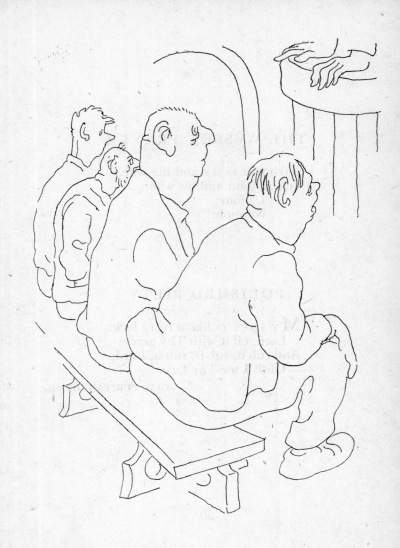

BRIGHT SPARK!

A DISSENTING MINISTER, at the end of a week of missionary effort, prayed:

"And if any spark of grace has been kindled by these exercises, O, we pray Thee, water that spark!"

THE SOUL–DAY SONG

GOD BLESS THE Master of this house
    And bless the Missus too
And all the little children
    Around the table, too:
Around the table, true good man,
    And happy may you be,
Sing Father, Son and Holy Ghost
    And life eternally.

A ROYAL METAMORPHOSIS

A PRESBYTERIAN MINISTER, called on at short notice to officiate at the parish church of Crathie in the presence of Queen Victoria, was so transported by the glory of the occasion that he burst out with the prayer:

"Grant that as she grows to be an old woman she may be made a new man; and that in all righteous causes she may go forth before her people like a he-goat on the mountains."

TAILPIECE

Pray God, by hook or crook,
Impiety to mend,
And help us, than this book,
To make a holier end.

Amen.

Printed in Great Britain by
The Camelot Press Ltd., London and Southampton